WALKS IN THE
FOREST of BOWLAND

Tony Ovenell

FREDERICK WARNE

Published by
Frederick Warne (Publishers) Ltd
40 Bedford Square
London WC1B 3HE

First published 1983

Cover photograph by Dave Pigott

Publishers' Note

While every care has been taken in the compilation of this book the publishers cannot accept responsibility for any inaccuracies. Things may have changed since the book was published; paths are sometimes diverted, a concrete bridge may replace a wooden one, stiles disappear. Please let the publishers know if you discover anything like this on your way.

ISBN 0 7232 3070 6

Phototypeset, printed and bound by Galava Printing Company Limited, Nelson, Lancs.

Contents

For Heather, George and Andy, the best of companions ...

'So long as a draw breath, a'll ne'er forget yon dale.
Owd fears cem out i aw that derk like sters.
O'er heead i t'sky there were these errie cries.
An there were a sense o bein pried on frae t tops aboon
bi fooumless black foourms again aw t Nowt behind,
gret Blash Boggarts o sterleet or the neet murr figures
o wer fogotten cheeldhood, Raw Eead an Bloody Boouns ...

                                        ...an we knew
then we'd done it, we were safe, we wouldn't dee affter aw —
not yet at least — an what's moour we'd aw foour crossed Bolland.

*Printed with the kind permission of Eddie Flintoff
from his dialect poem 'Crossing Bowland'.*

Acknowledgements

Many people, wittingly and unwittingly, provide help and information for a guide of this sort, but I must acknowledge here that I have relied time and again, on Jessica Lofthouse's books about Lancashire, both for information and for inspiration. Her knowledge of Bowland is unique and encyclopaedic, and my debt to her work is great. I must thank my colleague in the Royal Liverpool Philharmonic Orchestra, Dave Pigott, for his superb cover photograph, and for the diligence with which he sought this picture. Lastly, I thank my wife for her help, encouragement and advice, and for putting up with 'Bowland' day after day.

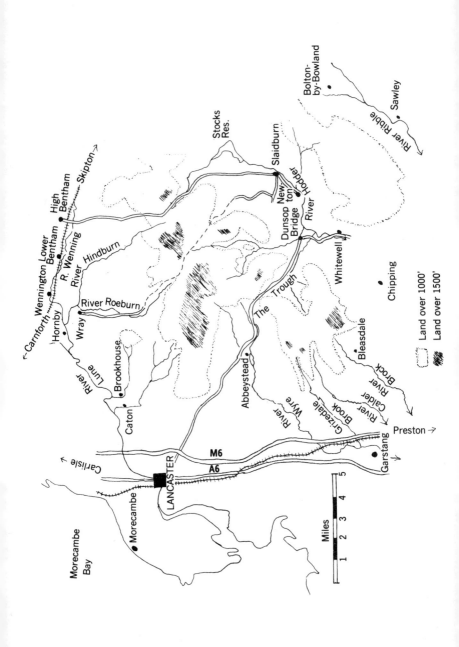

Introduction

This is the first walkers' guide to cover, as a whole, the magnificent Forest of Bowland, a little-known Area of Outstanding Natural Beauty of some 300 square miles in North Lancashire. It is a region of wild upland country, open moorland, deep cloughs and fertile dales, sprinkled here and there with charming villages and lonely farmsteads, all rooted deep in history. Much of this area, particularly towards the North and West, consists of windswept gritstone moors with weirdly-shaped peat hags and rough mat grass, which provide Pennine-style walking. Towards the South and West, however, in and around the area of the ancient Royal Forest, the landscape is softer, more wooded, built on limestone and watered by the idyllic river Hodder and its streams.

Geologically, the area is an outcrop of the Pennines, but it is separated quite distinctly from them and, because of this, offers the walker frequent and quite outstanding panoramas of the surrounding land: the neighbouring Pennine summits, the beautiful Lancashire Coastal Plain and Fylde Peninsula, Morecambe Bay and Furness and, beyond, the craggy outline of Lakeland.

This guide is divided into two parts. The first part consists of a selection of eight separate walks of moderate length in straightforward country—mainly the pastureland which adjoins the higher ground of the Bowland Fells. The second part consists of a four-stage long-distance walk over these more demanding fells, dropping down to the surrounding villages for the night's lodging. It is possible for the enterprising walker wishing to explore the area more thoroughly to link some of the separate walks with the long-distance 'Bowland Round'.

Historical sketch

The shape of the Bowland landscape which we see today was largely created by the ice which moved down from the Lake District before it melted, about ten thousand years ago. It smoothed the contours, and its meltwater carved great cloughs like the Trough of Bowland. After a warmer period, the landscape became clothed with plants and trees and, a little later, man appeared. An early Bronze Age timber circle can be seen at Bleasdale on the first stage of the 'Round'. The people who built it were probably semi-nomadic.

The Romans found a network of Iron Age tribes across the North of England, and they then built a great fort at Ribchester to control these primitive people. From here, Roman roads emanated—the Salter Fell Track on the third stage of the 'Round' may be one of them. After the Romans came the Angles, a lowland-loving people who began to clear the land and left us such place-name elements as 'ton', 'ham' and 'clough'. They were able to co-exist with the later Norsemen, who invaded from the West in around 900 AD, due to the latter's love of upland country. The Norsemen left us elements like 'thwaite', 'beck', 'keld', 'laithe', 'garth', and 'gill', all common in Bowland.

The earliest mention of the area by name was in the Lancashire Pipe Rolls of 1102, where it is referred to a 'Boelanda'. It is later referred to variously as 'Bouland' or 'Bochlande', 'the land by the bow', which probably means 'the land by a bend in the river' (Ribble). The name of the area is locally pronounced 'Bolland'. By the time of these references, the Normans had established themselves, villages were developing and individuals were beginning to emerge as Lords of the Manor, particularly the family of Robert de Lacy, who remained Landlords until 1311. They created launds or hunting parks, and stocked them with deer, and Bowland gained the status of a Royal Chase. Slaidburn became the capital of this 'Foris' or hunting land, and a court was set up (the courtroom still survives) for trying, amongst other things, offences against 'venison and vert' (vert was brushwood). The Middle Ages saw a period of great disafforestation and the establishment of 'vaccaries' or cattle-breeding farms. These tenant farmers were the ancestors of the yeoman farmers who, through the centuries, tamed the forest landscape and built themselves such sturdy settlements as Blindhurst in Bleasdale and Lickhurst Farm in Little Bowland.

A word about religion. Non-conformity is strong in Bowland. George Fox, the Quaker founder, made a famous ascent of Pendle Hill in 1652, and preached from the top. Various followers founded Quaker schools in the area, and Tarnbrook in Wyresdale was a centre for felt hat making—the type the Quakers wore. Other Non-conformist sects sprang up during the early 1600s, and a number of independent chapels appeared at this time. Even some of the Anglican churches have the plain, modest simplicity of the chapels, for example the former St Anne's church, tucked away in Littledale. Pendle, has a connection with witchcraft. The Witches of Pendle were put on trial in Lancaster in 1612, and were taken there by way of the Trough of Bowland, a dark cleft in the fells with a rather brooding atmosphere.

The industrialisation of the nineteenth century touched Bowland only superficially compared with the rest of Lancashire. The village mills (those at Calder Vale and Chipping are but two), which now seem almost quaint in their rural surroundings, must have had a quite devastating effect on the lives of the people at the time, especially on those fairly substantial communities in remote parts, for example Bleasdale, which existed partly or even mainly by weaving and spinning by hand. The remains of some of their sturdy cottages can be seen here and there.

Today farming, forestry, water collection and a little tourism give Bowlanders their main employment. There is local industry in some places, such as Berry's well-known chair factory at Chipping. The villages seem to be faring relatively well in the rural survival stakes. Their proximity to the rest of populous Lancashire must help them a good bit, but so too do their own folk—honest, friendly people with a strong streak of independence.

Map Notes

Key

– – – – –	path
▬▬ ▬▬	road
....	other paths and tracks
–·–·–·–·–	railway (++++++++++ on general map)
⊥⊥⊥⊥⊥⊥⊥⊥⊥⊥	fence
∞∞∞∞∞∞∞∞∞∞	wall
〜〜〜〜〜	hedge
〜〜〜〜→	stream or river
v v v v v v v	power lines
↑	deciduous)
⋔	) trees
	coniferous)
⛪	church
▪	building
▲	trig. point
△	cairn or summit
₀°₀°₀	boulders
�	crags
S	stile

10

G	gate
KG	kissing gate
FB	footbridge
YH	Youth Hostel
P.O.	Post Office
(8)	route miles

The maps in this guide should be used in close conjunction with the relevant OS maps. Their detail is not exhaustive, but is provided particularly at places where confusion might arise. The OS maps required are:

1: 50 000 sheets 97, 98, 102 and 103

1: 25 000 sheets SD 44, 54, 55, 56, 64, 65, 66, 74, 75 and 76.

For Walks 1 to 8 in Part 1, you ought to have the OS 1:50,000 maps, and clothing and footwear to cope with cold, wet weather and rough, boggy ground. A compass could also be useful. For the Bowland Round, Part 2, you must have at least the 1:50,000 maps, compass, wind and waterproofs, spare food and clothing, boots, and an emergency kit including first aid, whistle, torch and survival bag. You will then walk with an easy mind in the foulest of conditions.

The maps are based upon the Ordnance Survey Map with the permission of the Controller of Her Majesty's Stationery Office, Crown Copyright Reserved.

Every effort has been made to ensure that the walks in this guide follow rights of way and areas of public access. Neither the author nor the publishers can accept responsibility for those who stray from the Rights of Way or Access Areas.

Part One

EIGHT WALKS IN THE FOREST OF BOWLAND

OVERWYRESDALE AND ITS TWO STREAMS:

Walk 1   Abbeystead, Marshaw, Tarnbrook, Abbeystead

7 miles

OS sheet 102 Grid ref. 563544

With the fells of Wyresdale, and the Ward's Stone summit (the highest in Bowland) as a magnificent backdrop, this gentle and straightforward walk explores the countryside of two delightful little rivers, the Wyres of Marshaw and Tarnbrook, before they merge to become one. From Hind Hill, a good vantage point at 875 feet, one can gaze all around at Bowland's wild and sombre fells, the least known, least explored of any in Northern England.

For notes on Abbeystead, see 'A Bowland Round' Stage 1, page 40.

In Norman times, when the Forest of Wyresdale stretched right down to Pilling Moss, near Fleetwood, Marshaw was a much more important place than now. In the same way as Whitewell and Slaidburn had Swainmote Courts to administer the laws of Bowland Forest, Marshaw too had its Mote Houses for the same purpose. It also had an inn, the Cawthorne Arms, named after a wealthy gent called Mr Fenton-Cawthorne, who created the Abbeystead estate. He built himself a lavish, highly romantic and hopelessly impractical house, Wyresdale Tower (now a ruin), and finished up bankrupt. The estate was sold to Lord Sefton in the 1880s. The inn was the social centre of Wyresdale life for generations, the site of the annual sheep fair and agricultural hirings, as well as the haunt of journeymen, respectable and otherwise, who used the Trough road to come and go from Yorkshire.

For notes on Tarnbrook (5), see 'A Bowland Round' Stage 4, page 59.

This walk can be extended to Dolphinholme using pleasant Wyreside paths (distance 3½ miles).

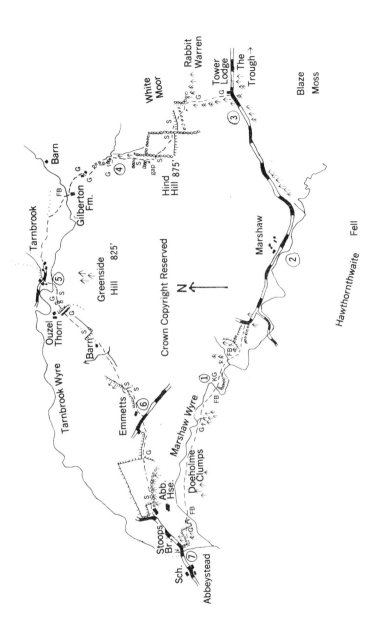

Rabbit Warren

White Moor

Tower Lodge

The Trough →

Blaze Moss

Barn

G

④

G

Gilberton Fm.

FB

S

S

gap

S

S

Hind Hill 875'

③

IG

G

Tarnbrook

Greenside Hill 825'

Marshaw

Crown Copyright Reserved

N

②

Hawthornthwaite Fell

Ouzel Thorn

⑤

G

S

G

Barn

S

②

Tarnbrook Wyre

Emmetts

S

S

⑥

Marshaw Wyre

①

FB

KG

G

G

FB

Abb. Hse.

S

Poeholme Clumps

Stoops Br.

S

G

FB

Sch.

⑦

Abbeystead

13

CALDERVALE AND NICKEY NOOK:

Walk 2　　Garstang, Oakenclough, Grizedale, Garstang

10½ miles

OS sheet 102 Grid ref. 493452

This walk takes a good look at two attractive tributaries of the Wyre, which find their way into the main river just north and south of Garstang. They are the Calder and the Grizedale, the first called river, the second, brook—a rather unfair distinction since they are equally small streams, with only momentary claims to importance, one as a mill stream, the other as a reservoir supplier. *En route,* the fascinating rural mill-village of Calder Vale is visited and later, something of a discovery for those of us who are not Fylde folk, the hideaway charm of Nickey Nook.

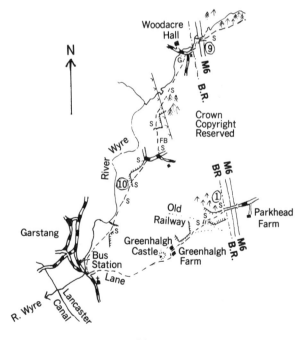

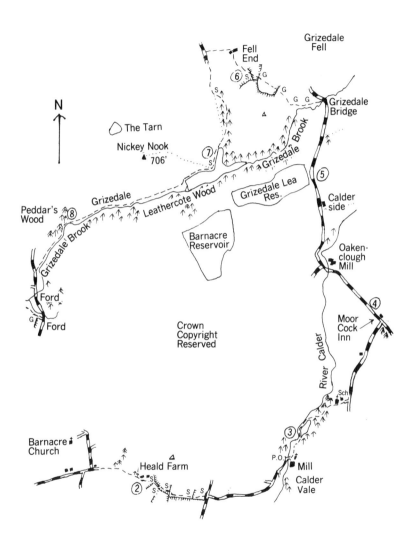

N

The Tarn

Nickey Nook
▲ 706'

Grizedale
Fell

Fell
End

⑥

⑦

Grizedale
Bridge

Grizedale Brook

Grizedale Lea
Res.

Grizedale

Leathercote Wood

⑤

Calder
side

Peddar's
Wood

⑧

Grizedale Brook

Barnacre
Reservoir

Oaken-
clough
Mill

Ford

④

Ford

Moor
Cock
Inn

Crown
Copyright
Reserved

River Calder

Sch

③

Barnacre
Church

Heald Farm

P.O.

Mill

②

Calder
Vale

15

Garstang is a pleasant little place, welcoming and friendly, with its four pubs and its busy market town atmosphere. It has a long history which well pre-dates the Domesday Survey. Eckwall says that the name is Old Scandinavian, and comes from 'Geirr', a spear, and 'Stong', a pole, and suggests that the words may refer to a boundary mark. At one stage, the Earls of Derby were its overlords, and it was they who built Greenhalgh Castle in 1490. Some of the castle tower still survives. The conspicuous church, south of the Wyre bridge, is the Roman Catholic one, built in 1858. The parish church, built in 1770, is tucked away to the West of the town, and is quite plain and simple, thoroughly within the style and taste of the place and period. In front of the Royal Oak (Robinson's beer) is what is left of the cobbled market square with its market cross, erected in 1754. Opposite is the town hall, built in 1755, and full of character, and round the corner is a real Lancashire feature, a clog-maker's shop.

Both mill and community at Calder Vale were founded by the Jackson brothers in 1835. Richard and Jonathan were proprietors of the cotton mill in the village, whilst John ran the paper mill, upstream at Oakenclough. They were Quakers, and had an idealistic vision of Calder Vale as a model village: no inn, but a temperance hotel with a reading room for the betterment of the villagers; all the houses to have gardens, and the people encouraged by annual competitions to keep them in order. Model villages can be rather artificial places, but not Calder Vale. With the advantage of a lovely wooded setting and a working mill, it would never occur to you that the place was conceived all-of-a-piece rather than having evolved naturally. Half a mile above the village is the church (interestingly, the Methodist Chapel is right in the village centre) built in 1883, and quite large. Next door is the school, very much alive.

The Moor Cock Inn is an excellent place for a rest, with good food, good beer and a lovely outlook.

Autumn is the best time for Nickey Nook, when the trees are a riot of russets and golds; the natural-looking reservoir adds to the beauty of the scene, whatever the season. Why not jog up to the OS column on Nickey Nook Fell? The effort is more than rewarded by the view, and it might help to shake off the torpor induced by lunch at the Moor Cock! There is no path off the top in our direction, only a steep bracken-clad slope, ideal for rolling down.

Woodacre was 'Wedicar' in the old records. It is an ancient manor, formed when Wyresdale Forest was being cleared. Somewhere near here there is an old spa well, but where?

LITTLE BOWLAND AND THE HODDER VALLEY - PART 1

Walk 3   Chipping, Burholme, Newton, Whitewell, Chipping

15 miles

OS sheet 103 Grid ref. 622433

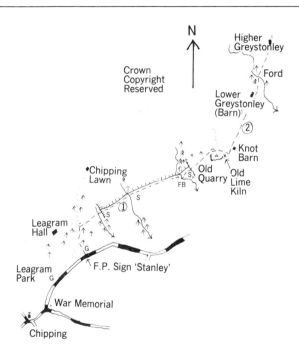

This is the first of two closely related walks from Chipping. They both explore Little Bowland and the valley of the river Hodder. This one has a little more climbing and some magnificent views, and is a good alternative route to Slaidburn from Chipping for those walking the Bowland Round in bad weather.

For notes on Chipping see 'A Bowland Round' Stage 1, page 43.

The name Leagram Park might be derived from an Old Scandinavian word, 'lathegrim'; 'lathe' meaning a blaze to indicate a road, and 'grima' meaning a mark on a tree to indicate a boundary. The Park has a long and involved history. From Norman times it had been run independently of the rest of the Forest of Bowland, though it too eventually came under the direct authority of the Crown. The Master Foresters of the time (often absentee earls and such-like) were allowed use of the Park by the Crown, and they made money out of it by confining and fattening deer, charging grazing rights for cattle and horse breeding. At this time, the Park was enclosed by an eight-foot-wide ditch, four feet deep and extending for five

miles, reinforced with oak palings. The deer could leap over this 'pale' from the outside, but it kept them there very satisfactorily, once they were in. Jessica Lofthouse reckons that there are traces of the ditch on the ground around Park Stile, Park Farm and Buckbanks Wood (names obviously closely associated with the Park), and a morning's work spent searching for it might well prove interesting and successful.

Later on, Henry VII leased the Park to two local families, the Sherburnes and the de Hoghtons, who were, unfortunately, arch-rivals — always poaching deer from each other, and generally causing trouble. It was the Sherburnes, however, who managed to gain outright possession of the Park in the end. When Elizabeth I gave it to her favourite, the Earl of Leicester, the Sherburnes discovered that he wanted to sell, and got in quickly. The Park has thus remained in the hands of the Sherburnes and their descendants right up to present times.

Road signs to the east of Chipping and around Doeford bridge refer to 'Little Bowland'. Where is Little Bowland? The name actually applies to the wedge of land bordered on the east by the stretch of the river Hodder between the Doeford and Burholme bridges, and on the north and west by the fells and by that famous Leagram Park ditch. It is worth remembering that, up until 1974, land east of this stretch of the Hodder was in Yorkshire; but, in reality, the area has always been something of a place apart — perhaps never more than in the days when chains were placed across the road from Chipping to discourage strangers. Happily, attitudes to visitors are rather more positive these days!

From Fair Oak (a maze of new and old buildings) you approach New Laund Hill, and then the path disappointingly skirts its base on the Hodder side. Nobody would begrudge you a quick detour to the top of this limestone knoll for the view which, on a fine day, is fabulous. There your gaze will penetrate the heart of the area which, on the map, is called 'Bowland Forest High'. Middle Knoll is there, easy to recognise because, from wherever you look, it always seems to be in the middle. The Dunsop Valley is channelling your gaze towards it, and on the west is Staple Oak Fell, on the

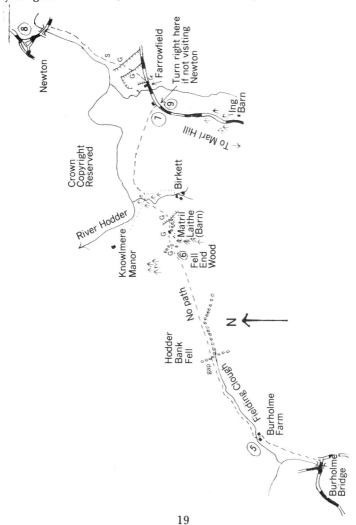

east, the fell with the loveliest of names, Beatrix. Below all this is the incomparable beauty of the Hodder, a word coming from the Old Welsh, and meaning 'peaceful water'. What name could be more apt?

Burholme is just a farm now but, centuries ago, was a good-sized hamlet — ridges and foundations of other buildings are there to be seen.

Hodder Bank Fell is the roughest section of the walk, rising to over 700 feet. The path is marked as being on the north side of Fielding Clough, but often the south side is easier. When you reach the col between Hodder Bank Fell and Birkett Fell, aim for the gap between two small plantations. Matril Laithe, a barn with a fine name, is your goal.

Newton is an optional extra, but a good place for a lunchtime halt (if you decide to keep going up the Marl Hill road, the Whitewell Inn would be another excellent refreshment post, but 1½ miles further at this stage than Newton). On a sunny summer's day, a cool drink in the garden of the Parker's Arms, which looks down to the Hodder and up to Waddington Fell, is just the thing. (Sadly, no real ale, but good food.) Newton was an early centre for Quakerism in Bowland; the 'Bolland Meetings' were held in the Friends' Meeting House, which dates from 1767. There are some lovely old cottages here in Newton, and an unspoilt, homely atmosphere which even Slaidburn does not match.

Note for wet Bowland Rounders — the footpath to Slaidburn follows the north bank of the Hodder, and is signed from Newton Bridge (1½ miles).

Above Seed Hill, the first of a series of massive wrought-iron kissing gates is reached; splendid things, requiring some skill in opening.

Whitewell is a well-known beauty spot, at a point where the Hodder runs by the church and inn beneath slopes overhung with trees. 'The Inn at Whitewell' is an old-fashioned country hotel, very ancient in parts, where residents can fish for trout and salmon in the hotel's own stretch of water. More to the point, there is a bar suitable for booted walkers, with real ale and superb food. It also does afternoon teas.

Stakes is a fine Jacobean T-shaped farmhouse, with the peculiarity of two doorways on the vertical section of the T; one north, the other south. It stands at an ancient ford crossing the Hodder. If the river is low, there are stepping stones for a dry crossing; otherwise, off with the boots and socks! At times of full spate, the alternative route to Chipping should be used, as in Walk 4.

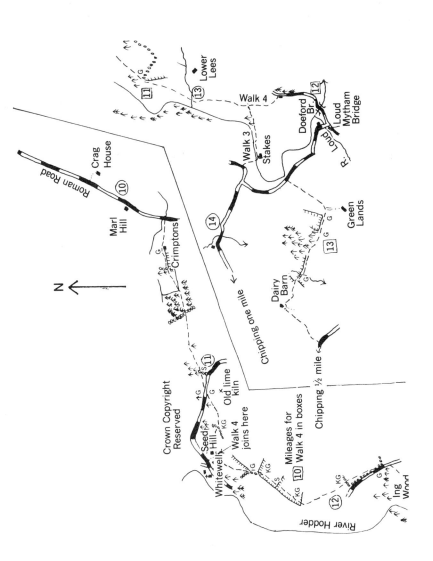

N

Roman Road

Marl
Hill

Crag
House

⑩

Crimptons

G

Crown Copyright
Reserved

⑪
S
G

Whitewell
Seed
Hill
KG
Walk 4
joins here
Old lime
kiln
G
KG
S
G
G

KG

KG
⑫

River Hodder

Ing
Wood
G

Mileages for
Walk 4 in boxes
⑩

Chipping ½ mile

Chipping one mile

⑭

Dairy
Barn
G

Walk 3
Stakes

Doeford
Br.

R. Loud

Loud
Mytham
Bridge
⑫

Walk 4

⑬

⑪

Lower
Lees

⑬
G
G

Green
Lands

LITTLE BOWLAND AND THE HODDER VALLEY - PART 2:

Walk 4   Chipping, Hareden, Dunsop Bridge, Chipping
14 miles

OS sheet 103 Grid ref. 622433

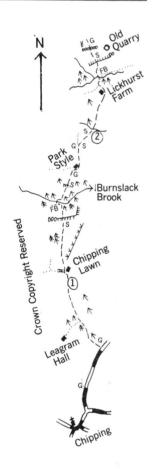

This second look at Little Bowland and the Hodder valley is just as enjoyable as the first, but a shade easier. There are good views of the valley, and a superb one of the high Bowland Fells from the slopes of Mellor Knoll. Refreshment stops are well provided for.

For notes on Leagram Park, see Walk 3, page 17.

Lickhurst Farm sometimes does teas and snacks 'for hikers only'; for once, discrimination in our favour!

Dinkling Green, also known as 'Dinkley' or 'Inkling Green', together with Whitmore, is a remote vaccary. (The latter is on the 1,000 foot contour). Do not go up to Whitmore, but turn right past some hen houses where hundreds of fortunate Rhode Island Reds scrap about freely.

Dunsop Bridge has a post office and shop, and some extremely pleasant surroundings.

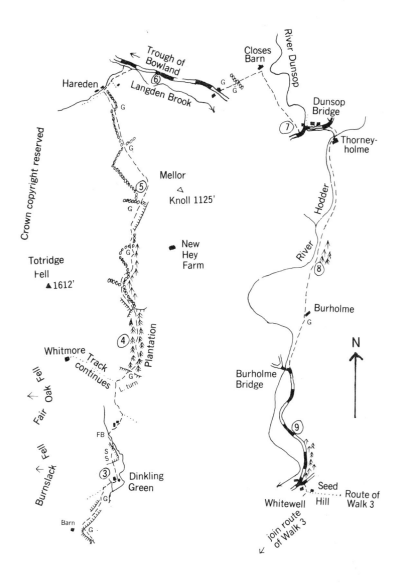

Trough of Bowland

Hareden

Langden Brook

Closes Barn

River Dunsop

Dunsop Bridge

Thorney-holme

Crown copyright reserved

G

G

⑥

⑤

Mellor

△ Knoll 1125'

New Hey Farm

Totridge Fell ▲1612'

G

⑦

Hodder

River

⑧

Burholme

G

Whitmore

Track continues

⑧

Fair Oak Fell

Burnslack Fell

Plantation

④

G

L. turn

Burholme Bridge

FB

S

S

③

Dinkling Green

⑨

G

Barn

G

Seed Hill

Whitewell

Route of Walk 3

join route of Walk 3

N

FROM HODDER TO RIBBLE AND BACK:

Walk 5   Slaidburn, Sawley, Bolton-by-Bowland, Slaidburn

14½ miles

OS sheet 103 Grid ref. 712525

This is a good day's walking around the picturesque countryside and villages of the south-eastern corner of Bowland, giving splendid backward views to the Bowland Fells, Ingleborough and Pen-y-Ghent. All this country used to be in Yorkshire, and there is more than a touch of dales flavour about the broad, tree-speckled landscape with its tight-patterned fields, peaceful villages and river-dominated valleys.

For notes on Slaidburn see A Bowland Round page 49.

On the 1:25,000 OS map, Broadhead Farm is interestingly called 'Cockshutt's Part', with Broadhead Farm placed ½ mile to the south east. After Skelshaw Farm comes Fell Side. At the time of my visits the remains of half a century's farm machinery lay astride the track to this farm, and the whole thing was a disgrace. If people littered their suburban back gardens in this way, there would rightly be an outcry, so why should those responsible be allowed to get away with it in our infinitely more precious countryside?

Easington Fell is but one of three names for this hill. It is also named Grindleton Fell and Harrop Fell, and what you call it depends on which side you are looking at. Very often in Bowland it is the slopes of a fell which have the names—summits are of interest only to walkers, and there have not been too many of these.

Sawley (the name comes from Sallow, a type of willow) is situated beautifully at a point where the fast-flowing river Ribble is overlooked on its south side by steep, wooded banks. A very pleasant scene it makes, and a good place for a picnic. Sawley is distinguished by the remains of a Cistercian Abbey, which date from 1147. The Abbey had a 'preposterously' short nave and, in fact, the building appears to have been wider than it was long.

There are some nice old cottages in Sawley, and some rather unhappy recent additions in the form of suburban-style houses, but saddest of all is the incongruous extension which threatens to engulf the old Spread Eagle Inn (now Hotel). If you want to eat or drink here, perhaps it would be as well to remove your boots to avoid soiling the carpet!

24

A lovely river valley walk now follows, to Bolton-by-Bowland, and if you do want something good to eat and drink, which is also cheap, you are recommended to make haste there.

Bolton-by-Bowland is a gem of a village, well-known but not in the

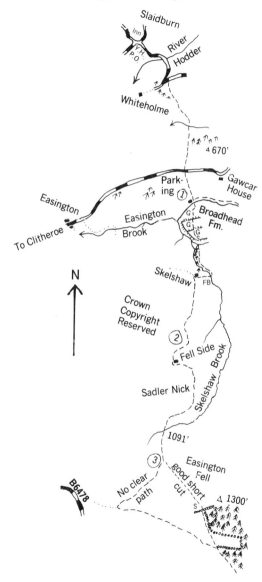

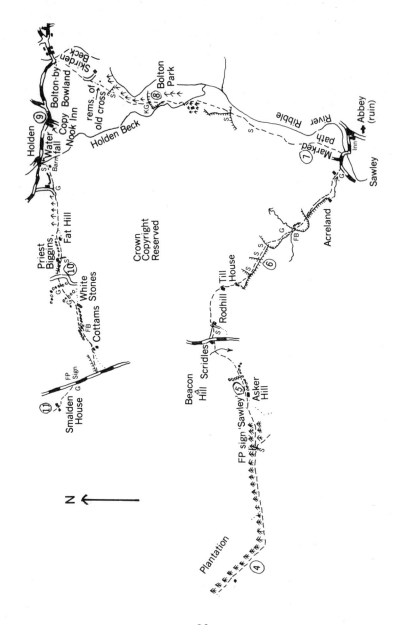

26

least spoilt. There are some fine buildings, particularly Primrose Cottage and Alder House. The church matches the beauty of the village, and is basically late medieval. Sir Ralph Pudsay, Lord of the Manor of Bolton, and his descendants supervised all the main stages of the building, and Sir Ralph's tomb, carved in black craven limestone and showing his three wives and 25 children, is on the south side of the chancel. He died in 1468.

The village pub, the Coach and Horses, does simple food and occasionally Hartley's draught ale. Why not try your luck! Otherwise, half a mile west of the village is the Coppy Nook Inn for more elaborate food and Thwaite's beer.

On via Fat Hill and Priest Biggins, to the Harrop Farms lying in the shadow of the fell. Few of the gates hereabouts open, so climb near the hinges for greatest safety. Harrop Fold lies high and isolated but the last farm, Harrop Hall is certainly the grandest.

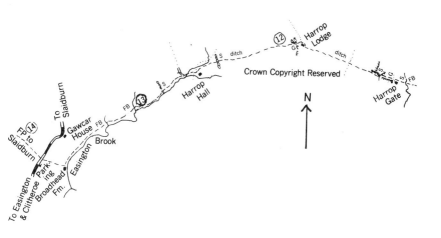

STOCKS AND BOWLAND KNOTTS:

Walk 6   Slaidburn, Stocks Reservoir, Bowland Knotts, Lower Croasdale, Slaidburn

13 miles

OS sheets 103 and 98 Grid ref. 712525

This is a fine walk to Slaidburn's northern skyline and back, taking in the drowned hamlet of Stocks, the invigorating climb to the viewpoint of Bowland Knotts, and the lovely paths which follow Croasdale Brook to Slaidburn.

For notes on Slaidburn, see 'A Bowland Round' Stage 2, page 49.

Hammerton Hall is mentioned in the Domesday Book, although the present building is Elizabethan. It was the house of the Hammertons, an old Bowland family with a reputation for great generosity. Strangely, their coat-of-arms shows three upright hammers although, in fact, the name comes from 'Hamor' meaning a hill.

The Church of St James at Dale Head is certainly worth popping into. It was built in 1852, using stone from the original church, whose foundations still remain on the bank of the reservoir near where the road to Clapham takes a sharp turn to the right. Apart from its remoteness and its peaceful atmosphere, the church has, hanging by its door, old framed pictures and cuttings of the village, now drowned, of Stocks-in-Bowland. With the pictures and descriptions of the twenty or so houses, the shop, the Post Office and the pub freshly in your mind, the view of the reservoir from the bridge, no matter how peaceful it looks, must be tinged with sadness when you think of all that has gone. Somehow, the pathetic little island with its telegraph pole and tree makes the scene all the more poignant.

Cursing our seemingly unquenchable thirst for more water, turn your back on Stocks, and throw yourself into the climb up Pike Side. At the top, no matter how inviting it may look, it is quicker to stick to the track, rather than to strike out direct for the OS column on Bowland Knotts. This is a small gritstone outcrop, whose summit is gained after an easy scramble over rocks. From here the view is ... well, I waste no more superlatives, my store is too low; see it for yourselves. In mist, Pike Side and Bowland Knotts are probably best avoided. From New House make straight for Parks Clough.

The paths back to Slaidburn are easy and delightful, providing many opportunities for lazy halts, picnics or whatever, by the charming waters of Croasdale Brook.

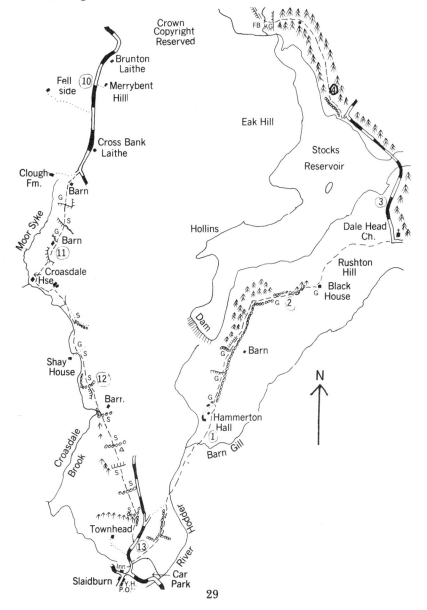

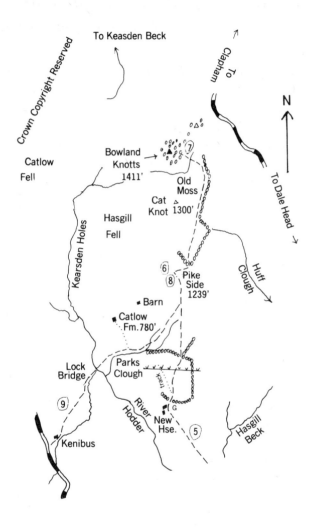

To Keasden Beck

Crown Copyright Reserved

To Clapham

N

To Dale Head

Catlow
Fell

Bowland
Knotts
1411'

Old
Moss

⑦

Cat
Knot 1300'

Hasgill
Fell

Kearsden Holes

Huff
Clough

⑥
⑧
Pike
Side
1239'

■ Barn

■ Catlow
Fm. 780'

Lock
Bridge

Parks
Clough

track

⑨

River
Hodder

■ G

New
Hse.

⑤

Hasgill
Beck

Kenibus

THE VALLEY OF THE HINDBURN

Walk 7   **Wray, Lowgill, Lower Bentham**

8 miles

OS sheet 97 Grid ref. 604676

Pick a clear, bright day for this easy walk, and you will be rewarded with grand views of some of the highest land in northern England — the Lake District mountains and Yorkshire's Three Peaks. In complete contrast, you can seek out the delights of the Hindburn, and find peaceful seclusion among the glades of one of Bowland's prettiest and least visited dales.

For notes on Wray see A Bowland Round page 52.

After gaining the farm road below Higher Broadwood, there follows a succession of sturdy dales farms, the grandest of which is Cragg Hall. Its beautifully decorated doorway, with the date 1693 above it, is there for all to see but, by all accounts, the inside is very impressive too, with oak staircases and dressed stone fireplaces, and rooms with breathtaking views. When you round the corner at Cragg Hall, one of those views will confront you. A little further and a defiant Ingleborough comes into view, much closer now than ever before on these walks, its vast bulk rising sharply from the ground to the north, suddenly giving way to flattened incompleteness.

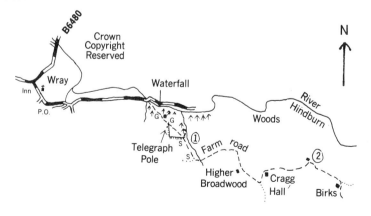

31

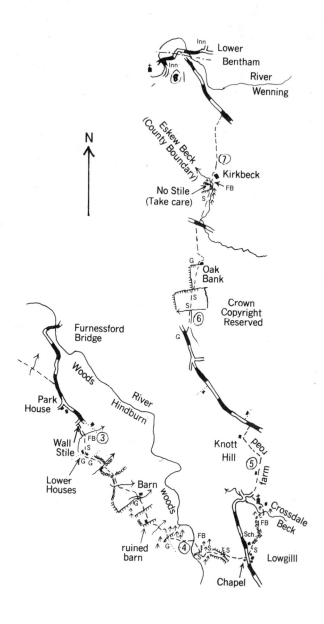

N

Inn
Lower
Bentham
River
Wenning

Inn

Eskew Beck
(County Boundary)

⑦

Kirkbeck

FB

No Stile
(Take care)

S

G
Oak
Bank

Crown
Copyright
Reserved

S

S
⑥

G

Furnessford
Bridge

Woods

River
Hindburn

Park
House

Wall
Stile

FB ③

S

G G

Lower
Houses

Barn

G

woods

Knott
Hill
⑤

farm road

Crossdale
Beck

FB

ruined
barn

G ④
S
S
S

FB
Sch.
S
S

Lowgilll

Chapel

32

The river Hindburn has never been far away and now, at last, it is reached and crossed where riverside woods give way to a meadow. The name should be pronounced Hīndburn, as in the word 'hind' (female deer), after which the river is named.

Lowgill thrives, despite its loss of shop and pub. It has a strikingly out-of-the-way atmosphere, which makes it all the more surprising, especially in these days, when you come across a flourishing school. You cannot but be envious of the fortunate children who grow up in these surroundings. Shortly after passing the school, you reach the Church of the Good Shepherd, aptly dedicated, and built in 1888, in which Pevsner finds much to praise. After crossing the beck, the path rises steeply to the church, and must keep the parishioners fit to a ripe age!

From Knott Hill and beyond, there are fine backward views of Upper Hindburndale and Botton Head. Above is the north-south Bowland watershed, and the birthplace of the river Hodder.

At Lower Bentham there are fairly frequent buses back to Wray, or indeed to anywhere on the Lancaster-Skipton route, and there is plenty of refreshment available.

LUNESIDE PATHS AND MOORLAND VIEWS

Walk 8   **Wray, Hornby, Brookhouse, Halton**

12½ miles

OS sheet 97 Grid ref. 604676

This is an easy and delightful walk, with a short climb to a lovely moorland viewpoint to add variety to the splendid Luneside scenes.

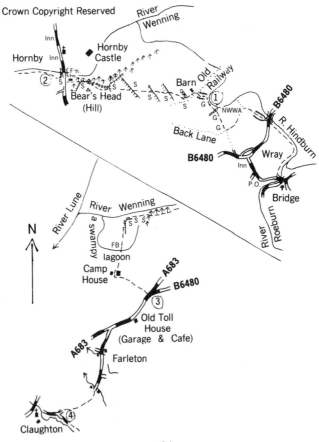

For notes on Wray see 'A Bowland Round' Stage 3, page 52.

Not far beyond Wray, Hornby Castle, a landmark for miles around, comes into view. The original castle dates from Norman times and saw much warring and strife over the next few centuries, due to the Scots invasions. It was the scene of a last-ditch stand by the Royalist cause in the area, but was eventually laid waste by the Parliamentarians after a tip-off about the one weak point in its seemingly impregnable defences. After further colourful episodes (all told in depth and amusingly by Jessica Lofthouse in 'Lancashire's Fair Face'), it was rebuilt in spectacular style in the middle of the last century. Apparently, a thirteenth century tower still exists amongst the Victorian romance — I say 'apparently' because the castle is not open to the public.

The Church of St Margaret in Hornby is interesting because it has an octagonal tower, built in 1514. Under this tower are fragments of an Anglo-Saxon cross known as the 'loaves and fishes' cross. No other such cross exists in England. Hornby has shops, a Post Office, a bank and two pubs, both selling local real beer and food.

Of Claughton village (pronounced 'Claffton' and derived from 'Klakkr', Old Norse for a hill) one can see little without making a small detour. It is worth it to see the oldest bell in England, dated 1296, in St Chad's Church, and the first instalment, a wing only, of Claughton Hall. This bit is now called Claughton Hall Farm; the remainder of the Elizabethan Hall is now situated in a splendid position 300 feet higher up the hillside, where it was shifted, stone by stone, in the early thirties. What a job! It is true, it has a terrific view, but was it really justified? To carve up an ancient building and move it about to indulge an eccentric fantasy like that would, these days, be considered sheer vandalism.

Having passed under the airborne hoppers carrying clay for Claughton Brickworks way down below, the ruin of Moorcock Hall is reached, and with it one of the grandest of panoramas. On a clear day you can see the whole of Morecambe Bay, with Grange-over-Sands standing out quite clearly; many Lake District peaks, including the Coniston Fells, the Langdale Pikes and Helvellyn; the Howgill Fells, the North Pennines including Cross Fell, Yorkshire's Three Peaks and, in the near ground, Lunesdale, looking green and lush.

Brookhouse has been overrun by Caton's determination to become another of Lancaster's suburbs. A pity, because the corner by the Black Bull and the church — called 'Rotten Row' — is attractive. The best thing about the pub, which sadly has been 'improved', is the superb Yates and Jackson's beer. Hot food is available.

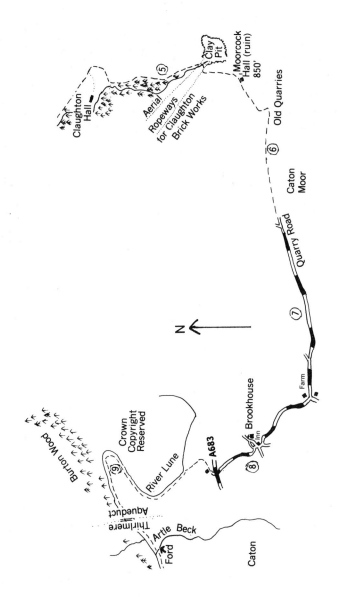

Claughton Hall

Aerial Ropeways for Claughton Brick Works

⑤

Clay Pit

Moorcock Hall (ruin) 850'

Old Quarries

⑥

Caton Moor

Quarry Road

⑦

Farm

Brookhouse

Inn

A683

⑧

N

Crown Copyright Reserved

River Lune

Burton Wood

⑨

Thirlmere Aqueduct

Artle Beck

Ford

Caton

Below Brookhouse, we rejoin the Lune, here sweeping and curving like a serpent. The Crook o' Lune is a sharp U-bend, west of Caton, but actually the name could describe any of the magnificent flowing movements made by the river around here. The low, woody, south-facing slopes provide a perfect backdrop to this noble river.

After an awkward section of the path, muddy and rocky in turns, we arrive at the disused Halton railway station, complete with faded sign. Turn left for the main road and the bus (Lancaster-Skipton route), turn right to cross the bridge for the village of Halton, which has much character. In the churchyard of St Wilfrid's is the famous eleventh century Halton Cross, which has fragments of a Norse saga inscribed upon it. Before this, the welcome White Lion Inn (Mitchell's beer) might satisfy your more immediate needs. From Halton, it is possible to follow Luneside paths all the way to Lancaster (2½ miles), if you wish.

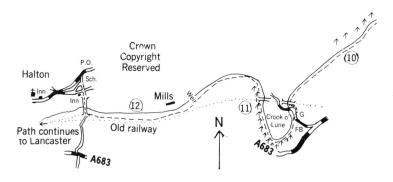

Part Two

A BOWLAND ROUND

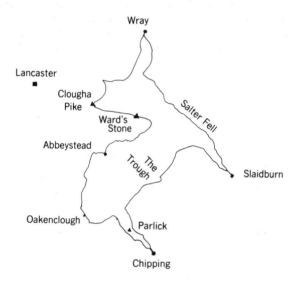

A 65-mile route over the

Bowland Fells

A BOWLAND ROUND

Introduction

This is a 65-mile 'circular' walking route which I have divided into
four stages, for ease of walking and for the convenience of stopping
overnight at pleasant and interesting places although, of course,
it can be walked in any way you like. The route concentrates on
roaming the accessible parts of the Bowland Fells, most of which
were, until recently, completely out-of-bounds to the walker. The
Ramblers' Association used to claim that this was the largest tract of
open country in England where public access was denied. Even now,
the land, which is either privately owned or the property of the North
West Water Authority or the Forestry Commission, is jealously
and assiduously guarded by gamekeepers for its grouse-shooting.
Over many years the Ramblers' Association and other individuals
made great efforts to gain access to this wild country for the walker.
Protests were organised, and mass trespasses took place. It was not
until the early 1970s that the Lancashire County Council managed to
negotiate Access Agreements with the landowners and, at last, some
(but by no means all) of this country has been opened up to walkers.
Countryside Rangers now patrol these 'Access Areas', and make sure
that people do not stray from them, and are aware of the bye-laws
and restrictions (see Useful Information). Do not get the idea that
these areas are regimented and patrolled, walkers marshalled and
told where to go. There are a few notices and signs, but I have
only ever seen two very friendly Rangers, and neither of these
was on the Fells. It is important, though, that walkers should not be
tempted to roam at will by the many challenges of this remote
and mainly trackless area. The Access Agreements can be termin-
ated at any time, and walking over prohibited areas can only
endanger these agreements, and inhibit any further developments.

Stage 1

Wyresdale, Bleasdale and the Vale of Chipping

13 miles

OS sheet 102 Grid ref. 563544

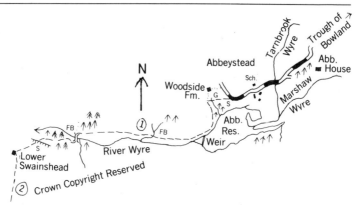

The first stage of this Bowland journey provides a fine introduction to the sights and sounds of the landscape which you will be enjoying for the next four days. The views are often extensive over the Fylde and the Lancashire Coastal Plain, but, if you are walking in the springtime, it is the sound of the curlew that will haunt your progress. The walking is gentle — through river meadows, field paths, ancient tracks and quiet moorland roads.

The round starts from Abbeystead in the heart of Over Wyresdale. Abbeystead's origins go back to the eleventh century, when a powerful Norman, Theobald Walter, gave land in Over Wyresdale to Furness Abbey for the establishment of a stead (farm) and chapel. The present church, half a mile from the village, dates from 1733.

The village itself consists of not much more than the school, the old post office and the big house, which all overlook the lake. It cannot have changed much over the years and has a peaceful, woody seclusion, such a feature of this lovely dale.

The rules of the school, founded by William Cawthorn in 1674, stated that the school master should be of 'sound religion, grave

40

behaviour, of sober and honest conversation, no tippler or haunter of ale houses'—let's hope the present one still is!

At the lower end of the lake, on the wall is a tablet which says that the lake was constructed in 1853 and holds 185,000,000 gallons. The big house, in the trees, was built in 1886 and belongs to Lord Sefton, landowner in these parts.

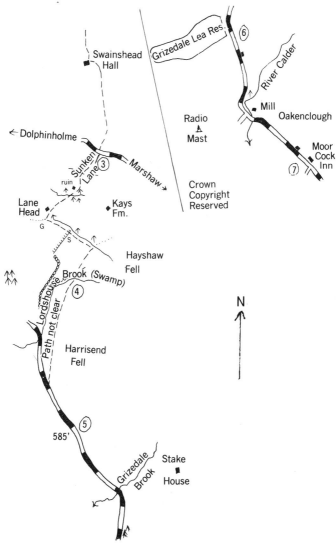

The section from Harris End Fell nudges the base of the forbidden fell country and it is hard surface walking (though often with good verges) all the way to Hazelhurst Farm. The burden of this walking can be considerably eased by a stop at the Moor Cock Inn, which sells hand-pumped Boddington's and Tetley's beer and good home-prepared food.

There is not much more to Oakenclough than the old paper mill and the pub. The real village is a mile downstream at Calder Vale, nestling in the trees and hard to get at. (See Walk 2.)

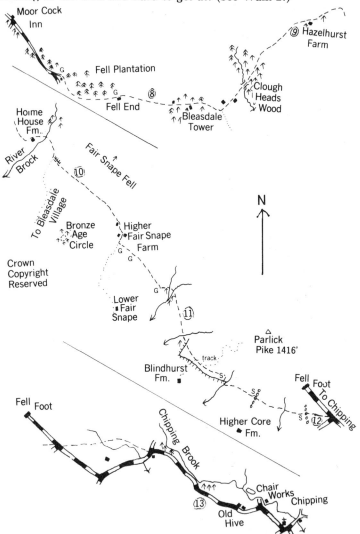

Bleasdale 'Tower', built in the 1840s, is a large country house set in wooded seclusion. 'Blesa' is Old Norse, and means 'a bare spot on a hillside', and there are quite a few of those around here. The Bronze Age Circle marked on the map is certainly worth a detour. It consisted of two circles, the outer a wooden palisade 150 feet in diameter, the inner, a ditch enclosing a burial mound 36 feet in diameter. Inside the mound were found two collared urns—these, together with part of the circle timber, can be seen in the Harris Museum at Preston. The circle is said to be 3,000 years old.

Fair Snape Fell and the ridge to Parlick dominate the final few miles of this first stage. Fair Snape is bulky and impressive, but it is Parlick that seems to preside over the surrounding country. The name of this shapely, broad-shouldered fell, says Jessica Lofthouse, comes from 'Pyre-lich', meaning a place of fire worship, and one can see that it would make a very good place for a beacon. The evening sun often catches this fell, and from Chipping it can look quite beautiful.

Chipping is a delightful little place. The name itself is Old English for Market Town, and was first recorded in 1203, although the village is much older than that. A church was first built here in 597, and full parish status was given in around 1040. The village as we know it was built on the wool trade of the seventeenth century, and John Brabin, a wool dyer, was Chipping's benefactor. On his death in 1683 he left money for a school and for poor relief. The school stands in Windy Street, as does a fine row of almshouses next door.

The exterior of St Bartholomew's Church was restored in the last century. Inside, the five-bay arcades are perpendicular and the north side has some carved heads making faces—fourteenth century or even earlier.

To the north of the village is Berry's Kirk Chair Factory. Built in the 1840s, it was once powered by water, and still has a beautiful mill pond. Furniture from the factory can be seen in the church chancel and also at the craft centre and Post Office.

The two Boddington's pubs in the village sell real beer; the third no longer does so. All the pubs do food, and the Sun, which is said to be haunted, has a stream running through its cellar. Its bar meals are massive.

The old Corn Mill is now a restaurant with a good reputation, and is called the Water Wheel Restaurant as it has a water wheel in working order. The telephone number is Chipping 553. And then there is Nuttall's, the sweet shop, selling delicious home-made ice cream. Chipping lacks nothing!

Stage 2

18 miles

OS sheet 102 and 103

The Bowland Crossing

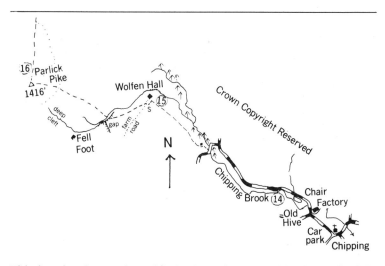

This is a lonely, at times bleak, but often superbly dramatic fell and moorland walk, crossing the upland area of the ancient Royal Forest, using Access Areas and traditional upland rights of way. There are very few of these rights of way in Bowland and, naturally, the ones which do exist are pretty old. One of those used here, the fell track from Bleasdale to the Trough of Bowland, was thought to have been made by foresters seeking a short cut between the forests of Bleasdale and Wyresdale. Apart from the brief encounter with the Trough Road, a tiny road often busy with tourist traffic, and two isolated farms, about which more later, the route remains quite solitary from the last of the Chipping farms to the first of the Slaidburn ones. Consideration should be given to the weather before setting out, mainly because, apart from the challenge, there would be little to be gained from a day spent almost entirely in mist and bog. There are better and more interesting ways to Slaidburn in such conditions (see Part One, Walk 3), and, for the inexperienced, the wild, pathless sections of the route could be a nightmare.

44

Wolfen Hall, the farm which stands right under Wolf Fell, has origins which go back to the thirteenth century. It was originally a look-out post to warn of wolves after easy prey on the newly formed vaccaries lower down the valley.

From the top of Parlick the view is superb, one of the best in Lancashire, but it is not a place for resting on your laurels, because you can see now where you have to go, and that too looks inviting. The little stretch of ridgeway linking Parlick and Fair Snape is a pure joy to walk. There is an inspirational quality about it that makes it (for me at least) stick in the memory and hold the affection to a degree which is far beyond its initial promise.

Having uttered words of caution about the weather on the previous page, I now say that all this section of walking can be hugely enjoyable in even the very worst that the firmament can fling at you. There can be an uncommonly violent westerly wind on the ridge which eventually buffets you the way you want to go. Then, once on the old track at Fiendsdale Head, surrounded by black bogs, the weather lowering and the air weighty with water, you glance at the map and see the names of Wolf Fell, Fiendsdale, Miry Ellis, Black Clough and you begin to wonder what drama there might be in store. Take care, though, and be sure that you know what you are doing with map and compass.

Langden 'Castle' is apt to disappoint—it is only an ancient shepherd's hut. A handy, if smelly, shelter nonetheless.

The valleys of Brennand and Whitendale, twins divided by Bowland's most endearing hill, Middle Knoll, represent for me the heart and soul of the matter. Their farms, which stand isolated, as

Fiendsdale Head 1470' △

Sign

clear path from Hazelhurst Fm.

Holme House

Holme Fell 18

R. Brock

Peat Hags

No path contourdale head

Crown Copyright Reserved

Fair Snape Fell 1674' 17

N

Nick's Chair

Blindhurst Fell

16 Parlick Pike 1416'

45

neighbours only to each other, have each tamed and worked the fellsides and valley bottoms in a way that has created a landscape of harmony and compelling beauty. Such partnerships of man with nature are rare these days. It is all too easy to overlook the element of sheer struggle which has brought about such a striking blend of wildness and cultivation. Sometimes it is hard to slow down, get out of your stride, forget the number of miles still to be covered, and take a good look at it all. Ted Hughes saw it like this in his wonderful poem of the Pennines, 'Crow Hill'.

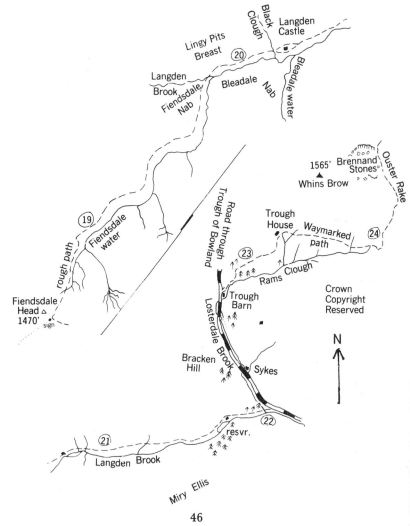

46

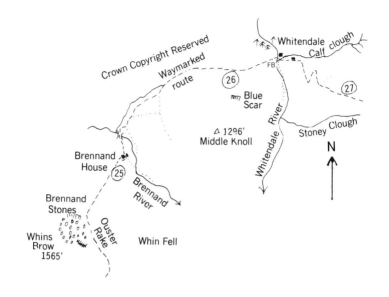

The farms are oozing craters in
Sheer sides under the sodden moors:
When it is not wind it is rain,
Neither of which will stop at doors:
One will damp beds and the other shake
Dreams beneath sleep it cannot break.

Between the weather and the rock
Farmers make a little heat;
Cows that sway a bony back,
Pigs upon delicate feet
Hold off the sky, trample the strength
That shall level these hills at length.

Buttoned from the blowing mist
Walk the ridges of ruined stone.
What humbles these hills has raised
The arrogance of blood and bone,
And thrown the hawk upon the wind,
And lit the fox in the dripping ground.

Reprinted by permission of Faber and Faber Ltd. from *Lupercal* by
Ted Hughes

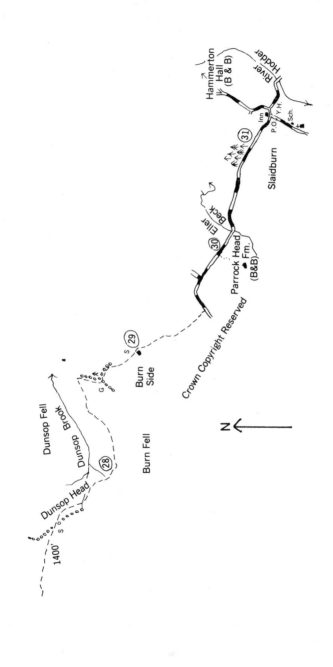

Hammerton
Hall
(B & B)

River
Hodder

31

Slaidburn

Inn
P.O. Y.H.
Sch.

Eller
Beck

30

Parrock Head
Fm.
(B&B)

Crown Copyright Reserved

29
S
Burn
Side

Dunsop Fell

Dunsop Brook

Burn Fell

G

Dunsop Head

28

1400'
S

N

The derivation of the name Slaidburn is not clear. It was 'Slateborne' in the Domesday Book, and so may have come from the Old English word 'slaeget', meaning a level pasture, a down or a sheepwalk. The village is near perfect, and a pleasant hour or so may be spent having a good look around.

The Church of St Andrew has a fine Jacobean rood screen, a good example of a three-decker pulpit and an interesting arrangement of box pews east of the screen. Here again you can see a more simple and direct approach to worship in the use of a communion table rather than an altar. There are also some old dog whips, used by the churchwardens when the farmers' dogs got rowdy.

The school next door to the church was founded in 1717 by John Brennand. Says Pevsner: 'a very pleasant building, orderly and not without substance'.

The Hark to Bounty Inn, or Dog Inn as it once was, is named after a hound of the local squire's named 'Bounty', who had a particularly recognisable voice. In the Bounty you can get a good pint of Thwaites' hand-pumped bitter in the bar, as well as seeing the old court room, seat of the ancient Courts of the Forest of Bowland. Have a look too at the river Hodder down by the old stone bridge—lovely throughout the whole of its course.

Sometimes referred to as the Salter Fell Track, this is a pack-horse route of great antiquity. It was used at one time by salt carriers for bringing salt, that valuable commodity, from Morecambe Bay to the isolated inland farms and villages. It weaves a rough and remote way through the wild fells of Upper Croasdale and over the watershed into Roeburndale, and it is possible, with luck, to have this whole eight-mile stretch to yourself. You are not just on the fells, you are right in amongst them, and so, perhaps, it is not without

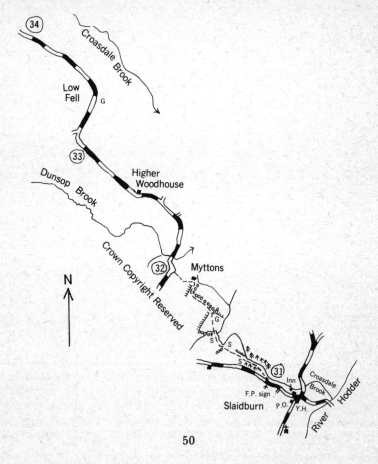

some justification that this has been called the finest moorland walk in the country. The beauty of it is that you can tackle it in any weather—once on the track only a genius could go astray. On a changeable day, with the mist, rain and sun coming and going, it is at its best.

Apart from the odd stony section, the track provides splendid walking. You can quickly establish a good stride, and then really bowl along enjoying the airy nature of it all.

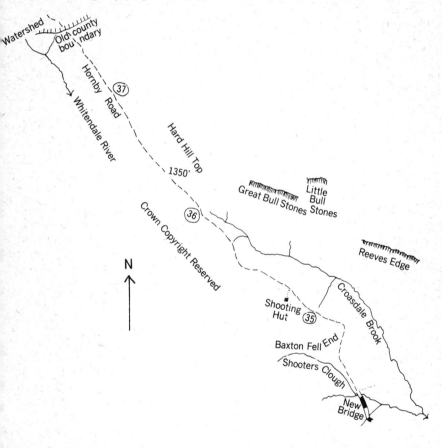

The rocky fell seen to the west is Wolfhole Crag—rocky in Bowland's terms, anyway. The ridge also with you on this side is Mallowdale Fell, culminating in the Pike, which is really best seen from the north. All the ground to the west eventually rises to the Ward's Stone plateau, out of sight just now.

51

Wray is a lovely spot—out of the way and full of charm. Its Norse name 'Vra' does indeed mean an isolated corner. The village street is most attractive with its terraced stone cottages and cobbled verges. A tremendous flood came in the summer of 1967, and all but

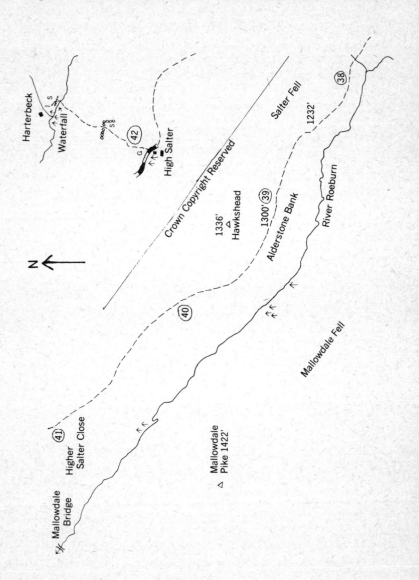

washed away some of the cottages and finished off what were, by then, already dying crafts and trades practised in the yards behind the cottages. Clog-makers, swill-makers (makers of oak baskets), bobbin-makers, even nail-makers once existed in this village. It also had its mill, producing silk; what a pity it has all gone. Some of the cottages have, however, been very well restored.

The George and Dragon in Wray is a comfortable and friendly place, which will be especially welcome to lovers of Mitchell's draught beers.

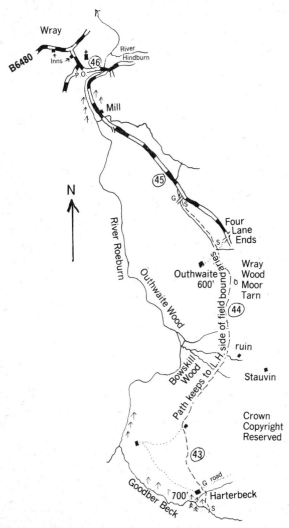

Stage 4

19 miles

OS sheets 97 and 102

Clougha and Ward's Stone

This final leg of our Bowland expedition provides a fittingly grand conclusion to the whole. There is a bit of everything in it, but, without doubt, the climax is reached with the climb to Clougha Pike and the traverse of the Ward's Stone ridge, which has all that a good moorland walk should have, and much, much more.

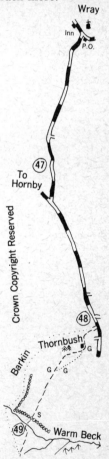

As you leave Wray, climbing Dick Brow, turn round frequently, if the day is fine, to enjoy the wonderful views of Ingleborough, Pen-y-Ghent and the rest of Craven. Passing the ancient farms of Thornbush and Winder (Norse settlements, almost certainly), it is the exquisite beauty of Roeburndale which strikes you, with the gentle point of Mallowdale Pike standing sentinel at its upper reaches, the Salter farms on the far side, and the old track which you walked the day before disappearing into the fells.

Deep Clough, the next farm on from Winder, is pronounced 'Deep Cloo', whilst, on the other hand, Clougha is pronounced 'Cluffa'.

Littledale is a tiny, forgotten valley, which sometimes seems overwhelmed by the steep fells which bear down on both of its flanks. It is also a place of great charm, especially in the Autumn, when colour is splashed about, seemingly with gay abandon.

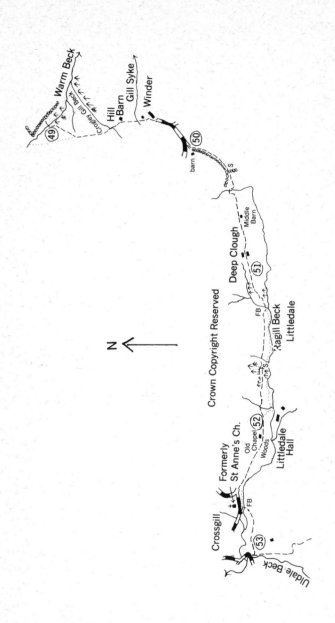

Warm Beck

Cogley Gill Beck

Hill
Barn

Gill Syke

Winder

49

50

barn

S

Deep Clough

Middle
Barn

51

FB

Ragill Beck

Littledale

Crown Copyright Reserved

N ←

Formerly
St Anne's Ch.

Old
Chapel

52

Woods

Littledale
Hall

Crossgill

FB

53

Uldale Beck

From Skelbow Barn your magnetic bearing on the summit of Clougha Pike is 208°. The first cairn you can see after Skelbow is on course, and is a good landmark. After this, cairns come regularly to left and right, but eventually you reach a fence with a large, well constructed cairn right behind it. The trig. point on Clougha is only just out of sight, but you cannot scale this fence. No matter, because you can follow it to the left, and will soon come to a stile, which is on a rough path. The route follows this path to the left (not climbing the stile) to Grit Fell (magnetic bearing 130°), and Ward's Stone. If, however, the weather is poor, or you are tired, or not confident or experienced, then your direction from here will depend upon where you want to be eventually. A magnetic bearing of 200° will bring you out at the Jubilee Tower (GR 542573) on the fell road to Abbeystead. A magnetic bearing of 260° will take you quickly to the summit of Clougha Pike, and you can then follow the path down by Rowton Brook, and so to Quernmore and Lancaster if you wish.

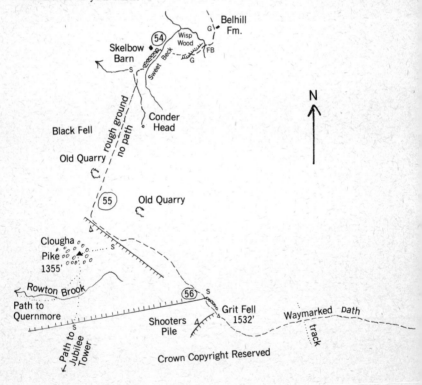

Crown Copyright Reserved

The title Access Strip is an appallingly prosaic piece of officialese for what follows. It sounds more like an airport runway than a name for one of the finest high moorland walks in the country. It takes four hours from Clougha to Abbeystead—four glorious ones.

The going underfoot is tough, the surroundings unrelieved in their bleakness, but the views and the feeling of being on top of the world, perhaps not even quite part of it, are what make this bit of walking so especially fine.

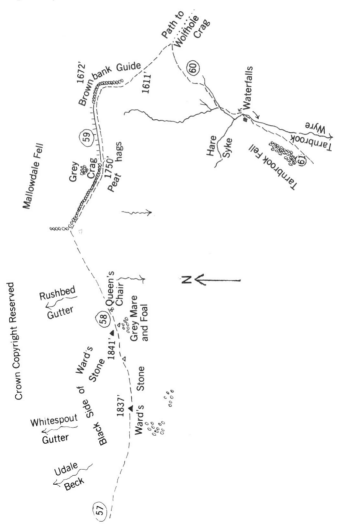

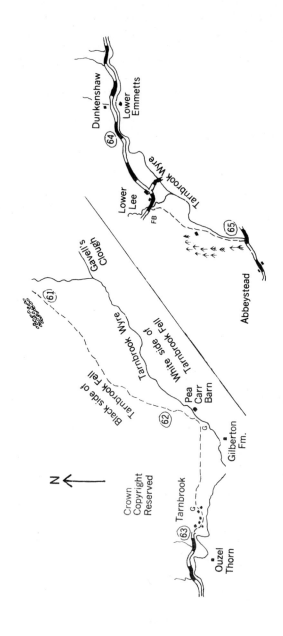

The summit of Ward's Stone consists of a huge plateau, with what few rocks there are gathered about the two Ordnance Survey columns, the easterly one of which is the higher. The rocks around this second column are called the Grey Mare and Foal, because of their arrangement, but this is not easy to see. Here and there, dotted about, are enormous peat hags, their crowns pushed up above the general level of the land and looking, perhaps, like strange craft drifting about in a barren sea of waste. The place has a weird, other-worldly beauty, which lovers of lonely moorland landscapes will not forget.

At the end of the Brownbank Guide it is not easy to pinpoint the place at which the path should turn sharply on a south-westerly course. It is better to turn sooner rather than later.

Tarnbrook is a little hamlet, so tucked away amongst the fells of the upper dale, that it hardly seems to have been touched by the modern world at all. Yet it was once a bigger and livelier place than now. It used to be a centre for felt hat and glove making, and Gornall's Farm, which used to be the Cross Keys Inn, was, before that, the home of Gornall, a Quaker hat maker.

Dunkenshaw (meaning 'the wood of the hedgesparrow') and Emmetts were both medieval vaccaries. Lower Lee House was also once an inn, built by the Haythornthwaites in 1694. In the big field beyond the footbridge at Lower Lee, look out for the Gad House, a long low building, very old, with pillars. It has protected cattle from gadfly for centuries.

If you make it to Abbeystead in time for the bus, the nearest pub for that drink you need to celebrate completing the Bowland Round is the Fleece at Dolphinholme. The bus will drop you at the door (the A6 bus routes are a further mile and a half away) and, with Mitchell's draught beer at its best, there is not a better place to finish up. If you have to go on to Lancaster, you can toast yourself in the other splendid local brews, Yates and Jackson's or Hartley's. If you have no time even for this, then at least try to get hold of a piece of local Lancashire cheese to take home. If you like it really strong, ask for 'tasty'. Lancaster itself is a marvellous old town, and it is definitely worth extending your stay to see it properly. But, to the 'Rounders' supping their Mitchell's at the Fleece, cheers and good luck!

USEFUL INFORMATION

Transport
Buses from Lancaster serve Abbeystead (infrequently) and Wray (Lancaster-Skipton route). Buses from Preston serve Chipping. Buses from both places serve Garstang. Slaidburn has a bus privately operated by Leedhams Garage, tel: Dunsop Bridge 237.

Accommodation
Abbeystead's nearest is at Bay Horse. There is a choice of B&Bs at Garstang, Chipping, Slaidburn, Bolton-by-Bowland and Wray, and there is an inn at Whitewell. Camping feasible on farmland with permission.

Access Areas
Limitations—no dogs, tents, stoves, fires or camping. Areas closed on some days during grouse shooting season—12 August to 12 December. Check with Ranger Service, tel: Forton 791075.

Further Reading
Books by Jessica Lofthouse—*Lancashire's Fair Face, Lancashire Countrygoer, Lancashire Villages* and *Three Rivers* all published by Robert Hale, and highly recommended.

Bowland and Pendle Hill by W.R. Mitchell, published by Dalesman. A motorists' guide with a lot of background.

A Bowland Sketchbook by A. Wainwright, published by Westmorland Gazette. Another beautiful sketchbook by Wainwright, with a good introduction, and three classic Bowland Walks.

Leaflet: 'Access Areas in the Forest of Bowland' published by Lancashire County Council.